CARELESS BOY BECOMING A SUCCESSFUL MAN

RODNEY STANBACK

I dedicate this book to all of the youth who has experienced hard times in life. To my parents, thank you for supporting me with everything in my life.

To my siblings and children, thank you for all you've done to be a big help to me. I also want to thank my family and friends for supporting me as I continue to walk this journey.

Last, but never least, I want to thank God for always being number one in my life. Thank you God for looking out for me even when I wasn't looking out for myself.

Prologue

Webster's Dictionary defines the word change *as to make or become different.* When looking back over several time periods in ones life, you can attest that part or all of you has changed. Sometimes when we define the changes we've made in our lives it was ultimately made because of a circumstance or by force.

When I first met Rodney, we both were in college, young and undefined. If I could sum up my first initial impression of Rodney in one word that would be *untamed.* You read that correct. He appeared to be wild and carefree.

Rodney was everything that I wanted to be at the time. I grew up in a sheltered household where college was my first taste of freedom. I could tell this was not Rodney's first rodeo.

At first glance, I could tell that he'd been through the trenches of life and college would provide the right change he would need to further exceed and excel in life.

By the second half of our first semester, I saw the change in Rodney myself. It was almost as if he'd made a complete 180 and I had an exclusive front row seat. Rodney was now a part of an all African American male organization, Black Male Initiative otherwise known as BMI and he was being a leader both in and outside of the organization.

His passions changed. He started to look different. He traded his baggy attire with more fitted clothing. He was now more approachable when walking on the infamous "The Bricks" a famous walkway on our college campus and instead of him being a carefree spirit, he had become a kind spirit. Everyone on campus liked Rodney including the faculty and professors.

During holiday breaks, Rodney and his twin brother Roderick where now exchanging the party scene with volunteering in our city by donating and giving back to the homeless. This was without doubt an extraordinary change that I was proud to witness.

Even now in our continued maturity, I still witness Rodney breaking barriers both personally and professionally. He's known in the community as a hard worker and influencer.

When he speaks people listen. People take heed to his advice and words of encouragement. He's active and involved in his church and with several youth organizations. He's also a mentor to disadvantaged youth in the community.

Rodney's story is truly a gem and worth the cliche saying, "Change is good" because truthfully, it is. As a reader, I hope that you will be inspired by Rodney's tenacity, his adaptability to change, what fatherhood taught him that the streets could not, and what change really looks like.

Rodney, thank you for being the change you wanted to see. Because of your efforts into changing for the better, you are an inspiration to men all over.

Chapter One

Being a man is more than just biology—it's a way of life and hasn't always been the way of life for me. Growing up, I lived in a two-parent household with my siblings. I have a twin brother named Roderick and we are complete opposites. Where my twin brother is more settled in his ways and mature, I'm more headstrong and can be stubborn.

While there are differences, we share some similarities. We both have a heart for giving, always looking out for the best interest of others and giving back to our communities.

Mostly, my childhood was great because my family and I didn't struggle. My father was in the military and stayed on the go but he made sure we were all good. My father took care of home.

Unlike most of my peers and those in my neighborhood I didn't have a reason to be a fuckup, but yet and still, *I fucked up.* I'll go into more details later.

I grew up in a rough neighborhood in Indianapolis with an even rougher father. My father was strict and wanted the best for his children. My family wasn't rich, but weren't poor and both of my parents made sure we had every want and need fulfilled growing up.

My father had a good reason to be strict. While at the time I didn't see or understand that my father wanted all of his children to make something of themselves and not go down the wrong path majority of the neighborhood kids went through.

My father had plans for his children that included excelling in school and someday going into college or the military. My father also made it known to everyone in the family: You will succeed.

That was a motto he planted and instilled young with my siblings and I.

While my siblings where busy trying to be the perfect students and kids at home, I was busy trying to be mischievous and get away with any and everything I could without my father knowing.

When my father was away in the military, I got away with any and everything. I was busy being the class clown and tough kid on the block. When my father was back around and in the city, I was a complete different kid.

Every time I got into trouble, especially at school I knew I could get away with it because my mother couldn't believe that her baby boy would do such things.

This day, my mother believes that her child can do no wrong. I'll touch more on that later.

However, when my father was in town and trouble found me, I got caught like a kid in the candy store. There would be no such thing as denying it or trying to talk my way out of it because all my father had to do was give me this look and I would immediately confess.

Every grown up with children knows the look I'm talking about.

It was as if my father had this hold on me. He just knew whatever I was doing was wrong. The man had eyeballs in the back of his head and knew I was up to no good.

I recount my childhood with my father because as a father, I now get what my father was trying to do and how I wish I could go back and redo some of my experiences.

I didn't have to grow up in the streets because of the family background I came from, but I choose that lifestyle. Again, let me repeat: *I did not have to grow up that way. I chose to.*

While growing up in the streets was a choice for me, it forced me to grow up faster than what my parents wanted. While my family was still trying to mold me and keep me as a young boy before fully experiencing life, I was out living what I thought was my best life.

I had inquisitively created this bad boy persona both in the streets and at school. However, my home life was the complete opposite especially when my father was home. There was no such thing as a bad boy Rodney at home. I was just Rodney, and that was that.

As a kid growing up in the Stanback household, my parents expected to be on your shit 24-7. Whatever the law was in the house was how it was no matter what.

If my father or mother gave us a chore to do, you did it without question. If they told to be in the house by a certain time, you came in the house by that time with no questions asked.

My father expected and wanted the best from his children so he and my mother created a structure for our family home. Now I'm in my late 20s and as a father I have a greater appreciation for my father.

When I was in school, I did not take it serious. School was boring to me. I didn't find it of interest because I didn't know what I wanted to do or what kind of career I wanted to pursue. Instead of trying to find an interest for my education, I found trouble to make the lesson or school day seem more interesting.

One particular day while at school and looking to start trouble, I did just that. I remember sitting in my desk ready to plot out my next move. I had my planned mapped out perfectly—*a bomb threat*.

I was so tired of school I wanted, no I *needed* a way out. What better way to do that than with a bomb threat? The perfect idea.

I proceeded with my plans but my parents weren't too happy with me especially my father. No ass whooping in the world could make my father get over what I did that day.

I couldn't deny it but the plan I had concocted was a genius idea for me. I had systemically thought of how to construct a bomb threat just to get out of class.

Looking back on that experience, I wish that I'd applied myself much more to my education instead of trying to get away from it.

Just as I had concocted the bomb threat, I could have taken that same energy and applied it towards my education.

Being in trouble with the law is what would later draw me towards wanting a career in law enforcement. I'll go into more detail about that later, but what I will say is learning to trust law enforcement was a process.

Thinking back on that bomb threat incident reminds me of another similar situation. When I was in middle school, I attended Franklin Central and I did the same thing. The only difference that time around was I felt out of place. Being the only Black kid in the class and general population amongst my peers was hard.

My middle school years attending Franklin Central was rough. During my time attending, someone accused of touching a white girl inappropriately even though I didn't do it. For the first time in my life I had experienced racism and accused of doing something I didn't do.

As a mentor I remind my youth you have to be very careful what you do because you can end up in jail.

Wishing I could have a redo in my education and life experiences is why I wrote this book. I wrote this book for every boy, teenager and even a man who may feel stuck in their life or what they've done is too great and they can't recover.

I'm here to tell you man to man: You can recover. One of the first steps you must take is realize you have self worth and that you are worthy. Read more about my journey in the following pages.

Chapter Two

I n 2004, I attended Ben Davis High School. It was a welcome change from my middle school years at Franklin Central because for the first time I was around people who looked like me.

When I started high school, my focus hadn't much changed since my days at Franklin Central. I was still being a fuckup, running around being reckless and living my best life at the time. In high school, my priorities still weren't school; I wanted to keep up with the latest Jordan's, and getting money.

The one thing that I am proud of from when I was in high school was my first job. I worked at Rally's across the street from my high school. Getting money was the mindset and I did it at all cost, even if it meant risking my job.

My manager at the time was a cougar and I was down with that. I'd never been with an older woman but I was open for the experience. One particular night after my shift ended, my manager called me to the backroom by the freezer where the food was located.

Once I made my way back to the freezer area, my manager stood there with a particular look on her face. After a few moments of an odd silence, she smiled at me and walked closer to me and began kissing me. I'm sure you can guess what happened next. This was a continuous cycle between her and I every time my shift ended.

Besides making money, girls also kept me occupied during my high school years. I didn't have much of a reason to skip school but I did hang out with girls after school. After school, you likely could find me at Chapel Hill Apartments at a female's house just chilling.

At the time, I had no worries and thought this was how life would be once I became a grown man, and out of my parent's house.

When it came to my education, it was a complete joke for me even still. While I wasn't skipping classes, I was however skipping assignments. I was failing in nearly every class I had.

I could care less of what was going on in the classroom. If it didn't involve girls, I didn't care. I hid my report card from my parents because my grades were terrible. I was ashamed of my grades and knew that my parents would not be proud of me.

If my parents would've saw my grades, there would be no going out for me on weekends. Hell, my parents would've also made me quit my job at Rally's. I could not let that happen. My twin brother and I had a fuck it mindset, and just threw out our report cards. We had to keep our lifestyle going on and didn't need a distraction.

In high school, I joined the ROTC program for something to do. The only cool thing about being in the program was being able to wear the uniform.

One day I talked a girl into hanging out with me after ROTC practice in the classroom. She agreed and once she got into the room, we had sex. We didn't get caught but it was the most exhilarating feeling I'd ever felt. Just knowing that I was doing something wrong, and didn't get caught.

Being promiscuous at such a young age was all fun and games until it finally caught up with me as an adult. If I could do it all over again, I would've waited until I was mature enough to realize the ramifications of having sex.

The truth of the matter is that anyone can have sex. But, it takes a mature individual to realize that sex is more than just physical.

When my daughters finally get old enough to have the conversation, I will certainly express that to them.

B y the time my senior year of high school came, I had to get my shit together. I didn't have enough credits to graduate, and my GPA was 1.6. After all of those years of hiding my report cards from my parents finally caught up with me. To all of the young men who are still in school, this is a lesson learned. Always be honest with your parents no matter how bad you think it may look. Even if you have fucked up, your parents will always be in your corner.

Even with my fuck up, my parents where still in my corner. I'll never forget the day my guidance counselor told me that I wasn't going to graduate because I did not pass the I-Step test. The counselor told me the only option I had was to take GED courses and he handed me the paperwork for it. It was at that moment that I realized all of my years of fucking around had finally caught up to me.

Although my grades weren't the greatest, I knew that I had made great strides to improve. In the back of my mind, I could not accept the final gate my guidance counselor was offering to me. The thought of getting my high school education through the GED route made my stomach turn.

Young men, going back to my previous statement, it's very important to be open and honest with your parents. I finally told my parents everything. I told them about my grades, and how bad my GPA was. Of course my parents were pissed at me, but we all banded together and knew what we had to do.

A few days after being handed what felt like a death sentence, my father went and talked to the School Board about a solution for me to graduate with my class. All prayers were needed and God certainly answered my prayer. My mother who was on her way to work, called me and told me that I was going to graduate.

May 30th, 2008 at 7 pm, I walked across the stage and got my High School Diploma. Not a GED, but a diploma. God was and is certainly still good. Everything was going well for me, until later after graduation I received a phone call that would rock my world.

I received a call that my favorite uncle, Gerald was shot and killed. I'll go into more details in a later chapter, but just as quick as my mood was up, it went back down.

Recounting my experience of almost missing out on being able to get my High School Diploma reminds me how important education is. To all of the young men, stay focused in class, do your homework and study for all of your tests.

Even if you're struggling academically, don't be ashamed to reach out and ask for help. Females will come and go, but your education is something that can never be replaced. Have an education opens the doors and windows to infinite opportunities.

Looking back on how I started a bomb threat all the way to throwing away my report cards, I knew better. Because I knew better, means that I could've done better. Even if you are bored in school, take it seriously because it's not forever. You're only in school for a short period of time, and you have your whole life ahead of you, due to what you put into your education. When it's all said and done, put your best foot forward when it comes to your education.

Focusing on yourself is also important. When you're in high school, you oftentimes believe the females you are with will be who you'll end up with forever. The truth of the matter is this is the time you should be focusing on your education, building a future, going off to college or picking up a trade. Females don't make your world —its what you make it.

In reflecting on my past, I also realize that being sexually active at such a young age wasn't worth it. Yes, I have a bunch of sexual memories and stories I can tell, but that's where it ends. At the time I didn't realize it, but I was placing my life in danger. I was at risk for more than just getting a female pregnant—I was at risk for contracting an STD.

Chapter Three

A t 18 I was not ready to be a parent. I think anyone is ever ready to be a parent that young, but somehow it happened and I had to get ready. I was still trying to live life on the edge just the way I wanted. That's why it was a surprise when my first child's mother told me she was pregnant.

You've got to be fucking kidding me, was all I could think about when she uttered those words to me. The relationship I had shared with her was one I took for granted. Although I wouldn't realize it until many years later, my relationship with her was the second most stable relationship besides the one I already had with my parents.

Ebony saw something in me. She wanted to push me to the limits to make me a better man, but I still played around and didn't value or appreciate her not only as my child's mother but my significant other.

We were young when we first got together. Ebony saw stability and someone to grow with while I just saw her as a sex toy. She saw me for me.

While she was busy seeing me for me, I was busy entertaining other females. There were other females willing to go places and do the things she would not do. She was boring to me. The girl who I thought was boring and plain was just what I needed.

Entertaining females other than the one you know for a fact deserves your fullest attention is easy if you have the mindset of a boy. Being a man compared to being a boy is all chemistry, but it's all relative.

As a boy you only see what's in front of you for now. And as a boy you aren't worried about being financially responsible or saving up for the future. With me having my first child so young, I was not prepared for anything except for the day at hand.

Growing into a man is a different story. My transition into manhood was a tough transition and took a lot to finally to get to this point. Once I finally made that change manhood took on a whole new meaning. I saw things differently.

I began to see what was ahead of me and prepared for the future and wanted to make sure I prepared for whatever was ahead. The transition into manhood took time, but it was worth it.

While Ebony was pregnant with our first child, I went off to college. Against the advice of my family I decided that going away versus enrolling in a local college would be the best solution because I wanted a better future and that was the only solution I felt would work. In looking back at how I didn't take my education serious, I wish that I would've worked something out with Ebony. But deep inside, I knew that having an education would take me far.

After going away for college for a few weeks, everything was okay and amid my transition my old ways began to creep back in. The temptation was there and there were too many females for me not to notice or look at it.

Being away in college was like being a kid in the candy story. There were too many options, and I had to have them all.

Meanwhile, while I was having fun away in college, Ebony was holding it down. She was holding it down as both parents and was taking care of the financial responsibilities while I was away having fun. She made sure my daughter had everything while I was trying to better my life.

During my first year of college I messed with Sarah Smith. We immediately hooked up, and that's all it was. Just sex. A repeating hookup. Sarah was everything I wanted—she was fun, sexually explorative, didn't nag me and she was down for any and everything. We had fun.

While I had a girl at home, Sarah also had a boyfriend so it was a win-win for us both. She wasn't sweating me with wanting a relationship because she already had one. We both kept our rendezvous on the low because we each had people watching us.

We both stayed in separate dorms close to each other which also worked out in our favor.

The all boys' dorm I stayed in was strict during the weeknights but more lenient on weekends. One particular night Sarah was up for some fun and so was I. Sarah and I created a plan for her to dress up like a boy.

Because I had a twin brother, it was easy for me to create a disguise for her so I gave her a set of my brother's clothes which looked a little different from mines.

One night during the weeknight, I met Sarah in the lobby area of my dorm and she was wearing an all black hoodie, fitted cap and baggy jeans. Because we dressed her like a boy, and she already had corn row braids, I checked her into the dorm with no problem. She kept her head down until we got into my room.

Once we made it inside of my dorm, we got right down to business. We had what I like to call a situationship, and it was everything I needed. I felt that I could talk to Sarah about any and everything. I thought she understood me and I understood her. We both wanted the same thing—fun.

We didn't take our situationship too serious because we both knew what it was, at least I thought so.

One day out of the blue, Sarah mentioned that she and her boyfriend was on the rocks and since things seemed to be cool between her and I she wanted to see if we could take things to another level. I did not see that coming at all.

Because I was already in a relationship with my child's mother, I knew I had to break things off seriously with her because we could no longer continue on with our situation.

Just when I was about to break it down to her, she then hit me with another brick with her next statement.

"I'm pregnant," As soon as she said those words, the room went black, and I wanted to pass out.

To make sure I heard her correctly, I asked her to repeat herself.

"You heard me, I'm pregnant,"

If I could cry at that moment I would've. Over the next few weeks I tried to come up with a solution to hide this pregnancy.

Deep down inside I was praying to God it wasn't my baby because I was barely taking care of my first child, let alone another child.

After a few more weeks passed the realization started to set in that I was about to be a father for the second time around I thought.

Just as I remembered the day Sarah told me she was pregnant, I remember the day she dropped another bomb on me.

"I lost the baby." There was a dead silence that stood the room still when Sarah said those words. I'd be lying if I said I wasn't relieved, but I felt for her.

The situation with Sarah and I was a prime example of how I needed to be more careful, but yet I still played with fire.

In 2010 after things settled with Sarah, I left college and moved back home to Indianapolis. After my last scare with Sarah, I got back on the straight and narrow path. That was until Brittany showed up.

While Ebony was in her last year of high school and taking care of our daughter, I met Brittany Tucker. Brittany and Ebony both went to school together called each other sisters.

Still missing the chase, Brittany was there to offer me what my baby mother still couldn't. Like Sarah, Brittany was fun, spontaneous and was very sexual. We first met at her Senior Skip Day and it went from there.

Like previous with Sarah, Brittany already had a situation and was just looking for some fun. We weren't trying to get into a serious relationship but somehow it happened.

Brittany and I became so comfortable with each other I would take her and Ebony to school in the morning. Ebony did not have a clue I was having sex with her friend.

Looking back over the experience of me bringing Brittany around Ebony was wrong and childish.

While everything was going well with Brittany and I and our little secret, the bomb came yet again.

"Rodney, we need to talk." Brittany said. I honestly thought Brittany wanted to break off our little fling, and I was honestly okay with that possibility.

But I was not prepared for her next statement, "I'm pregnant."

Chapter Four

Life has always been the best teacher for me, but some lessons I wish that I could have forgone.

The realization of Brittany's pregnancy finally settled in and I admitted everything to Ebony. I told her about how I had been having sex with one of her best friends. She was hurt, as she should've been. Even now the situation still very much affects Ebony. As a man I take full responsibility for it all. Back then, however I didn't.

After ruining the relationship for good with Ebony I still did my thing because I was a lost soul at that point.

During the summer of 2009, I attended the Indiana Black Expo, an annual event held in Indianapolis every summer. At the expo I met another girl named Wendy Jackson. As usual, Wendy and I got right down to business but this time around there wasn't any guilt because for the first time in a while, I was truly single.

The situation between Wendy and I was all fun until she got pregnant. She didn't want any children and had an abortion. I supported her in the decision because I already had one kid and another one on the way.

Growing up into a man took time and was a process that did not happen overnight. When I finally learned to put my childish ways behind me it opened up my eyes to see a whole new world and I finally realized that I was doing everything wrong and needed to be a better example to my daughter—and newborn who would soon come into the world.

The first step I took into becoming a man was realizing I needed to man up and put behind me my childish ways. Putting behind my childish ways included being more focused on my career and securing the bag for my two children.

After I began to focus on building up myself financially everything else started to fall in place.

The downside of building myself up financially was that I was always working. Between working two jobs and trying to build up it tired me, but it was all part of the plan for me becoming the man I needed to be for my two children.

While I was trying to start over and finally be a family man, I got knocked down again. On April 10, 2010 I was arrested with my cousin Loyce on the south side of Indianapolis.

I was sitting in my car listening to loud music with my cousin. An older white man came outside and told us to turn the music down. If he was being respectful, I would have done it with no issues, but he was being belligerent and racist towards my cousin and I. That's where the issue came from. Because I had my gun permit I had no issue with showing the racist old man who he was dealing with.

The older man eventually called the cops. Just when I saw the cops, I ran back into the house. The police would eventually get to my cousin and I.

Since I had a gun permit and my cousin didn't, he took a charge and was sent away to jail for two years while I spent less than a week there.

It affected my relationship with my cousin and we didn't speak to each other for years. I share this story because as a Black man I could have been put into the system for a long time by my actions. Making the right choices is very important especially if you have a family.

Believe it or not, it was this turning moment in my life I decided I wanted a career in Law Enforcement. Growing up, the thought of the police gave any and everyone bad vibes but I wanted to change that stigma.

I wanted people to see that not all police officers were bad, and there were good cops around. I wanted to be a good cop. So I took the next steps to make that happen.

Deciding to get into Law Enforcement was not an easy task, but it was something I wanted to do. I took the next steps by doing my research to find out how I could get into this career.

I took on a second job working with the Children's Bureau and it was me working with kids that really put into perspective what type of Law Enforcement officer I wanted to be.

I wanted to be the reinforcement for disadvantaged youth who were going down a wrong path by showing them a better way and that it's never too late to turn your life around.

Working at the Children's Bureau was just the start. It allowed me to mentor young boys all while befriending them yet giving them a different perspective on life.

Looking back on the experience and my younger years I wish that I would have taken it more seriously and been a part of a similar program when I was growing up.

B y the time I turned 21, life was still a little funny for me. I could finally buy liquor legally and I still wanted to hang out. I'd much rather hang out with my cousin YG, smoke weed and drink.

I had a good job, but I still wasn't ready. Instead of being focused on work and my children, there was still a playboy deep down inside of me.

I lived for the weekends. Back in the day there was a night club called Tremors and that was the spot everyone wanted to be at and I was no exception. Although a part of me was changing, there was still a little boy inside of me.

Instead of smoking weed and drinking at 21, there were alot of other things I could've been doing. Instead, I could've been building my credit and investing the money I was making into a business. Instead of doing the right things I should've been for my children.

I was more focused on tricking on the females and smoking weed. If I could take a moment to tell the young men reading this book anything, be more smart with your money.

I used to waste money on Coogi clothes every week at Lafayette Square Mall in Indianapolis every weekend. I wore so much Coogi that my nickname used to be Coogiman back in the day.

On Saturday mornings I'd foolishly stand in line just to buy the latest Jordan shoes. I could've been investing my money in the company instead. Back then it didn't make any sense to me, but the older I became it did.

Investing your money wisely is the smartest thing you can do. Who wants to be the old man who is broke and has nothing saved? Young men, it's important to realize your financial worth and making sure you are securing your future now.

If your job has a 401k program, invest in it. Even if your job doesn't offer any of those programs, you should still take a vested interest in your financial future. That's also part of the transition of stepping into manhood.

Chapter Five

Recollecting my memories of fatherhood and growing up on the West Side of Indianapolis brings back nostalgia memories. One nostalgia memory I have is my relationship with my uncle.

My uncle Gerald was a street man and everybody respected him.

While my uncle was a street man, he was the street man that would give you the shirt off his back. No matter what you needed or what you may have owed him, he looked out for everyone.

Uncle Gerald was the street man that would allow you to extend your credit if you know what I mean. He gave and gave, yet well respected and people knew not to take advantage of him.

We had a close relationship. He not only put me on game but he also taught me game I still carry with me til the day. That's why the day someone killed is a day that I'll never forget. My uncle's killing did something to my spirit I just can't seem to forget.

It was the end of my senior year in high school and what was supposed to be a joyous and happy occasion turned out to be a nightmare. A few weeks before both graduation and my open house to celebrate, my family and I got the most devastating news ever.

My family and I had learned that someone who killed him, was a so called friend. In the time leading up to my uncle's memorial service my family also learned the person responsible for his murder had a jealous streak going for my uncle.

It was supposed to be having my open house to celebrate graduation but I was celebrating the life of my uncle at his funeral. No kid wants to have that experience, but yet there I was having it. It was supposed to be a joyous occasion, but my family and I were in mourning.

The day of Uncle Gerald's memorial service still plays out in my head.

My uncle meant a great deal to my family, but he was a staple in my life and he was who I inspired to be as a person. Now let me clarify, I didn't want to be a street hustler like my uncle, but I wanted his personality. I wanted to be just as giving and caring as he was.

There are days when I often wonder what my uncle would think of the man I would eventually become. His approval meant a lot, and that's why I think about him a lot.

Thinking back over how much my uncle meant to me brings me to my next point: it's important to have people in your life who want to see you win and succeed.

As I began to make the transition from boyhood into manhood, that's when I'm reminded the importance of knowing your circle— my uncle also taught me that.

As a man, it's important to remember to have the proper influences around you. As you truly transition into manhood the way you think, act and ultimately turn into changes. It's very important to have the right people around you. Think of it as having your own personal life coaches or mentors in your circle.

We all need that group of friends who are there to tell you when you are wrong, lift you up when you're down and lends a listening ear in times of need.

Chapter Six

When I think back on how far I've come, I'm reminded of my past life and what I used to do. Back in the day, the thought of being with multiple women kept me going.

In my younger years, all I thought about was sex, so having multiple women allowed my fantasy to become a reality. While having multiple women was all fun and games majority of the time, it became stressful.

As I look back before I really began to turn my life around, I often think about my first child's mother and how all she wanted was stability, and a loyal man. It was all childish, and that was the least I could provide for the mother of my child, but I failed at it.

When my first child was born, I was not ready to be a father at all—I was still a boy. The thought of providing for my daughter was the furthest thing from my mind. Now days my kids are my pride and joy so if I could go back and have a do over, I would on that issue.

Although I wish I could have a do over on certain areas in my life, there are some areas where the tough lessons made me into the man I am today. I got caught up in a lot of dumb stuff, and some of it is quite laughable this day.

As I recounted the story about my uncle who was a great influence in my life, I'm reminded how I tried to sell drugs. I was a wannabe drug dealer all because it looked cool and I thought it was something I would be good at not knowing my foolish choice was putting my life at risk.

The thrill of being with multiple women also put my life at risk. I found this out quickly when I tried to have a threesome. It's hard enough trying to please one woman so pleasing three was a challenge. I don't think I'll ever be ready for that challenge again.

Thinking back on an experience I had in my younger years would be going to Club Inferno in Indianapolis and bringing back multiple African women to my house.

When I was in college I had always heard African women were wild and I was ready to test that theory out. While me and my boys where partying in Club Inferno I spotted an African woman out who was dancing wildly. After she finished dancing, I went up to her and spat my game to her.

"I think you're beautiful. Wanna have some fun?" I said to the mysterious woman.

She looked back at me and replied, "Can I bring a friend?"

Nothing else needed to be said, so I told her to bring her friend and follow me back to my house. Once we got back to my house, the mysterious woman and her equally beautiful friend got right down to it.

Both women had me going in directions I never saw coming. By the time we were all finished, they both drained me. Even as a young man at that point, I knew a threesome would not be for me again.

Thinking back on that experience, there were a couple things that were wrong: I didn't know either women's name, and what if I caught an STD?

If I could take a moment to really speak to young men all around, there are a few things I want to express heavily: Having multiple women is not the way. There are so many diseases that puts your life at risk to catch and it's not worth it.

There are over a hundred different diseases you're at risk for getting by taking part in sex with multiple partners. Is it worth it to you? Also, think about your future and take into consideration your children.

As a parent of daughters I had to take into consideration the future I wanted for my girls.

Somehow the narrative has changed when it comes to manhood. The youth I mentor think being a man means having lots of money, a good job, or a good car and plenty of women at a snap of the finger. The material things don't make a man—it's the character of a man that really makes a man a true man.

Growing up, I saw the men in my family including my uncles and both of my grandfathers have multiple women. From an outsider looking in, seeing the men I admired have plenty of women around gave me something to look forward to as I was growing up. Somehow this bad trait carried over to me as an adult. It was as if I was meant to be a ladies man growing up.

From being a ladies man to having the latest shoes, I had it made—or so I thought.

Chapter Seven

Hopefully, as you've been reading my story you've learned a few things about me. I hope that you've learned I'm a straight shooter and I have a past. Part of the lesson of boyhood to manhood I had to learn was accepting my past and that it's okay to have a past.

Accepting your past is just part of the stepping stone into manhood. Once you have accepted your past for what it was and what you can do to move forward not only shows growth, but it also shows maturity.

If I could turn back the hands of time and do things differently with each of daughter's mothers I would. I'm not saying I would get back with them, but I would've handled both situations more mature and respectful.

Looking back at both situations I wasn't the man I needed to be and I own and accept that.

With the growth I've had I have been able to show my daughters how a man is supposed to treat a woman. I make sure my daughters know they are both loved and that I'm trying to be the best for them.

They both don't have a doubt I'm the best and continuously striving to be better.

One day while having a conversation with a friend we were talking about our past and how far we've come along. In our discussion we talked about how we used to be, things we used to do and the people we used to hang out with. I was then reminded that some people I used to hang out with are no longer alive.

I thought about how my actions could've cost me my life. Taking part in reckless sexual activities with women could have caused me to have a disease or even worse, my life. I thought deeper about how my relationship with my children's mothers may not be all roses, but we have an amicable situation.

I'd like to take a moment to talk further about the relationship with my second born's mother, and just how far we've come and how I've matured.

When my youngest was born, everything was good for a minute, and then she was taken away from me. I was adjusting to fatherhood with my second child and then the storm happened. My daughter's mother went away with my daughter for almost four years.

Brittany had taken away my daughter away from my family and I because she could no longer handle we were no longer. She was a woman scorned.

Those four years were in deed a fight. I knew nothing. I tried everything to get my daughter back. During my battle I felt it was unfair. Here I was, a Black man trying my hardest to take care of my children after going down a slippery slope. I moved two steps ahead and got knocked down two feet deeper.

Once Brittany finally came back, we reconciled, sort of. I began messing around with her again, now knowing she had a boyfriend. We both were playing with fire and I did not mind at all.

Now I was messing around with Brittany again for several months, and able to see my daughter I was on cloud nine.

One day while out Brittany told me she was pregnant, but she didn't know if the baby was mines or her boyfriend's. The weeks leading up to me finding out the paternity of the baby was nerve wrecking.

I still remember the day it all happened. I've never been a fan of being amid drama but there I was. Brittany and I was hanging out at her house when her boyfriend at the time surprised the both of us.

He had a key to her place, and while the both of us were sitting on the couch just relaxing, in he came. He had a subtle look on his face. He was ready for war. Because I didn't want any drama, I politely got up, looked at Brittany and left. I knew this wouldn't be the last time I'd see her, but deep inside a man could only wish.

Until that point I'd been with a lot of women and have gotten myself in very uncompromising situations, but at that moment I knew I needed to do better.

A few weeks after that encounter with Brittany's boyfriend I finally found out the paternity of another child of mines. Turns out, I was not the father.

As I reflect over that period in my life I'm reminded of another stepping stone into becoming a man. I stepped into the zone of trying to get my daughter back into my life after her mother viscously took her away all because I didn't want to be with her.

This was also another very important lesson into stepping into manhood: know exactly who you sleep with. Sleeping around is all fun and games until a child comes into the picture.

I didn't take the time out to get to know her and as a result, I ended up going through a rough season.

Growing through that rough season allowed me to man up, and gain a better appreciation of practicing self-love. It also taught me how to pick better partners.

Chapter Eight

Growing up in the Stanback household, a lot of my relatives thought my family was well off. Not only my side of the family, but everyone also thought my father's brother Kevin was well off as well.

My cousins would make fun of me because they thought my parents were rich because of their careers. Although my parents weren't rich, they simply worked hard for what they have. Both of my parents didn't grow up in well-to-do neighborhoods. They both grew up in the ghetto and decided they wanted to have a better life when they got older.

Looking back over how I treated my education growing up makes me sad at times. Both of my parents made a lot of sacrifices to show my siblings and I a different way of life. As I mentioned in an earlier chapter, I didn't have to be a fuckup, I chose to be one.

My father is a great example of a man. He was strict and stern, but he meant well. Now that I'm much older and mature, I realize that my father is the kind of man I aspire to be like daily. He works hard, is always providing for our family and genuinely looks out for everyone around him.

It's truly because of my father that I strive to be better each day for my daughters. I can only hope when they start dating, their boyfriends will be an exact replica of their grandfather.

Not only has my father been a great example to me, but my mother has been as well. My mother has always showed a great deal of patience with me. Even while growing up and starting shit, my mother would always be there for me.

Even when I first told my mother I was having my first child, she was there for me. She was slow to judge me and always believed there was a good man deep down inside of me.

I'm proud to say that I have a great relationship with both of my parents today. It's because of them and seeing what they've accomplished over the course of my life that I was able to change.

My parents also instilled in me the importance of having a relationship with God. Without my relationship with God, I'm not sure where I would be. My parents made that a top priority for me and it's something that I won't ever forget.

Everyday that I wake up, I'm reminded that it was God's grace that woke me up to see another day that was not promised. I look at young men who are in the street and I oftentimes think out loud they are here simply because God granted them another day.

I did a lot of horrible stuff growing up and he kept me. Just like my parents, God has and never will give up on me. Now as a parent I make sure my daughters know and have a relationship with God. I want my daughters to know that God woke them up and everything they have was given to them by God.

Another valuable life lesson my parents taught me was the power of hard work. I didn't grow up waking up to the power being off. I always had food on the table regardless if I wanted to eat it or not. My siblings and I didn't go to school with raggedy clothes. We all had the best of the best.

The reason I work hard as I do this very day, is all because of my parents. I want to be able to leave a legacy for my daughters. I want to leave this Earth knowing I left my daughters financially secure.

I make sure that I teach my daughters the importance of saving and investing as well. I want them to grow into independent women and not having to depend on a man for anything.

Young men, it's very important to respect your parents. You may think your parents are boring, or don't know anything but they know a thing or two. Your parents only want the best for you, so if they tell you to do something, do it. Also, remember that your parents are not supposed to be your best friend especially when you're younger.

Your parents are in your life to help guide you and show you the right path to go towards.

If you think your parents are being mean to you, be grateful. Truth be told, your parents aren't being mean to you. They are just being the concerned parent they should be.

G rowing up, I tried to stay out of the Stanback household as much as possible. As an older sibling, it was my responsibility to look after my younger siblings but I wasn't the greatest at doing that, nor was I the best example. Looking back, I wish that I could've been there more for my baby sister Cara.

My baby sister Cara and I are the complete opposite. She's always worked hard in school, made good grades and even graduated High School without my parents having to intervene on her behalf.

While there is an age difference between Cara and I, I could've done a lot better. Because I was so wrapped up in my own world and head, I didn't think we had anything in common, which is why I never hung around her.

I mention my younger sister because she's an example of what growing up in a good household can do. My sister took the tools that were given to her by our parents and made something out of herself.

I'm very proud of my sister and the woman she is becoming. I have a better relationship with her now and I know with continued prayers to God, our bond will only get stronger.

Although this book is primarily for young men, there may be a young girl reading this book, and I want to share something with you as well. Don't let a boy try to sweet talk you into anything.

Instead, stay focused on your education and secure your future. Boys will always be around, but don't be in a rush to get to them. The world is a big place and as a young Queen, your focus and priority should be exploring this big world we live in.

Also, to the young girls, remember having sex is not important. Just because other girls in your school are doing it, doesn't mean you have to be a follow. Be a leader and not a follower. Lead other young girls to being something great in life.

Chapter Nine

During the many tests and trials I went through including putting my life at risk there was once source that kept me through. It was God.

1 Corinthians 13:11 reads: When I was a child, I spoke like a child, I thought like a child, I reasoned like a child. When I became a man, I gave up childish ways.

This scripture has a deep meaning for me. When my cousin Loyce was in jail from the situation I had gotten him into, he sent this scripture to me. I've been reading this scripture ever since.

Whenever I read this scripture, I'm always thinking of how I can continuously change my ways. As the scripture reads, when I was a child I did childish things. When I became a man I put away my childish ways.

My childish ways included having multiple women, getting women pregnant and not wanting to take responsibility and not standing up and owning up to my mistakes.

The irony of this scripture is that my cousin gave this to me when we were trying to heal our relationship.

This is one of my favorite scriptures more than just the obvious reason. This scripture also reminds me of my grandmother.

It's crazy to believe throughout my entire reckless behavior, God never left me. It's because of him that I'm still alive. God kept me alive for a reason and for that, I'm forever grateful.

During my childish ways, I knew that I needed to go to church, but I was always to hungover from Saturday night to make it into church on Sunday morning.

To my young men, it's important to attend church. Having a belief in God gives you the balance that you need to survive in such a cold world. God should also be the first priority in your life. When you choose to put God first, that's when you really start to live.

Once I finally started to put God first in my life that's when doors began to open for me. It wasn't until after I fully developed a relationship with him that I realized he was the missing piece in my life.

All of the women, money, cars and clothes could never compare to my relationship with God. I'm forever grateful to my family for introducing me to God.

My grandmother had a way with words and telling things like they were. She would not sugarcoat nothing no matter who you were. One day, while just checking in with my grandmother she asked me how I was doing. I gave her the response I thought she wanted to hear, but she could tell I was bullshitting her.

"Tell me the truth. How are you really?' She asked again.

I thought about my answer carefully before responded. I thought back over the last nine months and how much of a roller coaster it had been.

I explained what I'd gone through recently. I felt comfortable sharing my trials with my grandmother because she offered me a judgement free zone.

After I poured out my heart to my grandmother, she looked me in the eye and said, "Smell it before you taste it."

Because I was still young in the mindset, I assumed this meant something entirely different from what my grandmother was trying to convey.

I had a nasty mindset and literally thought my grandmother

meant to say just what she said. However, years later it would not hit me of what my grandmother truly meant.

As a grown man, I had to learn you have to look deep before you dive in. That includes women and career moves. Just because a woman looks pretty on the outside doesn't mean she is good for you.

Just because a career looks to be good and lucrative doesn't mean it's for you. All money ain't good money.

B y the time I turned 20, I had my first apartment. I lived on the West Side of Indianapolis in a complex named Westlake Apartments. The West Side of Indianapolis is where I grew up and that's where all of the action happened.

It wasn't until I got my first place when the females really started to come around. While I'd always been somewhat of a ladies man, having my own place just seemed to heighten the experience. I had a different female with me every night. I had one for Monday, Tuesday, Wednesday, Thursday, Friday, Saturday and I rested on Sunday's.

My cousin Quinton ended up being my roommate and we would split the bills. He was not only my cousin, but he was also my party buddy. He loved the women just as much as I did. Quinton was a great roommate because he managed his money much better than I did. Because my cousin was much better at managing his money, we never went without.

There was another person who was in my life at that time who was important. I have a half brother whose name is also Rodney. That's another story for a different book, but Rodney was my other partner in crime.

Rodney partied with me every night and we made sure the ladies had a good time as well. While I was enjoying myself, my roommate and cousin Quinton was starting to get frustrated with me.

While I had money for weed and liquor, I barely had enough money for rent. There were times my cousin had to cover my half of the bills. I remember a particular situation where my car was repossessed because I was being irresponsible.

Looking back, I was dumb as hell. There was no way in the world I was ready to be out on my own. I should've stayed home with my parents and saved my money. Because I was being hard headed, I learned a tough lesson.

To all of the young men reading, think long and hard before you decide to move out and get your own place. Make sure you are financially ready and responsible. The worst feeling in the world is working for something all for it to be taken away from you. That's exactly how I felt about my car when it was repossessed.

Of course if I could do it all over again, I would've managed my money better. Also, I would've followed the example my cousin Quinton was showing me.

Chapter Ten

T hinking back over my life I can say I'm blessed. Now I've my past, I want to take the next few pages to talk to men with daughters. Whether your daughter is young as 3 months old, or twenty years old your daughters need to know you love them.

As I described in the earlier chapters, I went from being a kid getting ready to head off to college to an overnight father.

When my first daughter was born, I was not ready to be a father, but I knew that gaining a higher education would help me on the journey to becoming the father I needed to be for my daughter.

I wish that it would have worked out that way but when I got to college I was like a kid in the candy store. There were multiple women, and I had choices.

Instead of focusing on the mission at hand which was getting a proper education, I was more focused on the women and having lots of sex.

Since my focus was more on the women instead of the books, in came Brittany The relationship between us was all fun and games until she got pregnant with my second daughter.

When she took my daughter away, it broke me as a man. For the longest I believed that I couldn't provide, and that I was a bad person.

The four years that my daughter and I were apart from each other was a fight I wish on no man. It took a lot of strength and tenacity to finally get reunited with her.

If I could say a few things to my daughters, I would want them to know that I love them both dearly. I would tell my daughters I didn't know the strength I truly had until I became their father.

My daughters Raniya and Ramiah both have my heart dearly. Sometimes I honestly feel I can't talk to them like I really want to. If they were boys, our relationship would be very different in how I approach them.

No father wants to think about their daughters dating and their interactions with boys. Once Raniya and Ramiah gets older and start dating, I will refer back to this book for them.

I hope they won't date until they are forty.

I also want to let my daughters know the importance of education because I didn't value mines when I was younger.

Having an education or a trade opens the world up to you for infinite possibilities. Although my daughters are still young, I instill this into them both and they have made me proud.

While education is important, I want my daughters to grow into women knowing their worth and value in society.

In my boyhood years I treated women like toys and didn't take into consideration their hearts. When my daughters grow up, I want them to know what is and not acceptable from a man.

I want them to know they should should expect to be with a man who genuinely cares about them and not just after one thing.

God has a funny sense of humor, because he blessed me with daughters.

Chapter 11

Growing up, I had a "fuck the police" kind of mentality. As a boy you could not tell me I would grow up working for the Law serving our community. Growing up on the West Side of Indianapolis, I viewed the police as the enemy because I saw how they treated the people in my community.

After leaving college I decided that I wanted to do something that would help the community instead of harming the people that lived in it. In came my decision to start a career in law enforcement.

I didn't jump into law enforcement right away but I mentored youth with my job. It was while working at the Children's Bureau when I realized my passion for mentoring youth—young boys in particular.

During my work with the youth I realized that my passion for at-risk young men was at high stakes and there was work to do.

These young men felt comfortable talking with me about their problems or issues at hand. They saw me as the non judgmental big brother and they listened to what I had to say. They actually listened.

These young men were going through some of life's toughest moments and I was there to experience it in real time with them.

My career at The Children's Bureau further solidified my decision of wanting to get into law enforcement.

But instead of wanting to get in to law enforcement for all the superficial reasons such as having a cop car and having a gun I wanted to change lives. I wanted to show my community and all other underprivileged communities that all cops aren't bad.

Looking back over my decision, I also thought about my friends. Would my friends still hang out with me when I became an official officer? Would they view me differently, or still see me as Rodney? These questions arose in my mind but then it hit me: I've got to do better for my children.

I knew that I needed to change my life for the betterment of my children. I could not be out in the streets selling drugs and become nothing. I needed to leave a legacy behind for both of my daughters.

I wanted my daughters to know their father worked hard for everything and didn't take the easy route for success.

Not only did I want my daughters to see my hard work pay off, I also wanted to have open and honest conversations with my daughters about my career. I even envision myself visiting my daughters at their school for career day to talk about my career.

When I think about the future and what it means to me and my family, I get excited because I'm a testimony of cleaning up what I messed up and starting life over again.

It's important for me to be an ally to my community. Just as I mentor youth at the Children's Bureau, I mentor outside of the workplace in communities and stepping into law enforcement has allowed me the opportunity to be the ally my community needs.

Being part of my community is also what has contributed to my growth. My twin brother and I make it a personal duty to give back to our community. We volunteer our time by giving food to the homeless, providing financially and just being a listening ear.

One thing our parents taught us growing up is the importance of giving back. Giving back to my community what motivates me to keep pushing to higher levels.

As an ally for my community and city I'm able to understand

the wants and needs of the community. As a law enforcement officer I want to better communities and let them know that all cops aren't bad. For me it's more than just being an officer of the law. It's all about stepping into communities that are voiceless.

As I look ahead into my future with law enforcement, I get excited. I get excited about the thoughts of helping my community and being that ally they truly need. To me it's more than just putting on a front for the media but doing it when the cameras are long gone.

To me it's all about being the source and changing the narratives of how people view the police. There are bad cops out there but I vow to be a good cop, looking out for my community.

In my continued conversations with my mentees I often make it a point to share with them the importance of law enforcement. With so much police brutality going on in society, I'd be a fool not to share with them what to and not to do when they feel threatened by an officer.

When I was growing up it was rough, but not as rough as it is for today's youth.

Today's youth have much more to deal with compared to previous generations such as bullying and even being exposed on social media. Our kids are committing suicide as a result from constant bullying.

To any young man who is reading this book and is being bullied make sure you talk to someone. It's important for you your voice to be heard because you are important.

Alternatively, if you are doing the bullying take some time out to think about your actions and how it's impacting the one being bullied.

In reflection, if I could go back to my youth and do some things over I would. I went from being a careless boy to a successful man. I'm living proof you can change with the proper direction and help. I had people in my corner namely my father who wanted to see me succeed and do my best.

While it was my fault I fucked up over the years, my father never stopped caring. I witnessed my father do things he preached to me including getting a higher education. My father knew what education could do, and he was right.

Also, if I could go back to my younger years, I would have showed more respect for police officers. Instead of thinking they were the enemy I would've tried to make allies with them so they could've helped my community.

Sometimes you don't know what you don't know until you don't know it and that was one of the toughest lessons I ever had to learn.

In looking back I laugh at the thought of how I couldn't stand the police, and now I'm becoming the police. Life has a way of changing things around wouldn't you agree?

Chapter 12

I'm not the same person as I was at eighteen nor am I the same person I was at twenty-one. Throughout each phase of my life I learned tough lessons. I learned about fatherhood, how to be a provider and how to go from being a careless boy into a successful man.

I'd be lying if I were to say it was easy. It was a journey to get to this point in life where I can proudly pull a young man to the side and mentor him because I've been there before.

I beam with pride whenever my mentees come back and tell me how much of an influence I've made in their lives.

Looking back over the life my uncle lived reminds me of the man he wanted me to be. Although my uncle was the neighborhood drug dealer, he looked out for the community. That's exactly what I'm doing. I'm giving back and sharing knowledge and life lessons all in one. It's truly a good feeling.

The more successful we become at developing our black boys into men, the more we become a threat to the world. I've learned that white men in fear us black men.

Once we have developed into a more woke mindset and have taken back our power, we are a threat to them.

No matter what situations or curves life throws at you, it's important to always think through it as a man. What would a man do? If you get yourself into a sticky situation, truly think it through with the mindset of a man and how a real man would react.

There is so much killing going on and things we see in the media probably has us scared, but if we stop and think about the background of those being killed it's because they didn't have proper direction or mentors in their corner.

As I reflect over my younger years, I think about how I was going down the wrong path because I wanted to and it was not a reflection on my parents, but me instead. I take full responsibility for being a fuckup.

Growing from a careless boy to a successful man meant that I took responsibility for my own actions. Making this transition also required me to hold those around me accountable.

In earlier chapters I talked about the death of my uncle and how that impacted me. A takeaway from my uncle's tragic death is that you must hold your circle accountable and if anyone is not living up to the expectation of being great, then you have to let them go.

Growing from a careless boy to a successful man means you are always growing. It's not okay just to be okay with being mediocre. Part of life is evolving and changing.

I took a leap of faith by deciding to make law enforcement a career I would take seriously.

Had I been okay with just getting by for my daughters I probably would still be right where I was years ago wondering why I can't get ahead. I took a chance on myself and it was the best thing I could've ever done.

When I pursued law enforcement, I had several people try to talk me out of it. I had several people label me as being on the enemies team. But then I started a conversation of how trusting law enforcement can change your life if you let it.

For many years I was convinced the police was the enemy and couldn't be trusted because of all the police brutalities going on in the country. After letting my guard down, I realized we need law enforcement as an ally. That was me changing the narrative.

Growing from a careless boy to a successful man meant that I valued my life. Now as a man I value my life and choose who I decide to let in my life including women.

No longer are the days of playing around with multiple women. Women are precious and should be treated as such and not a toy.

Being a man is not all about giving multiple women attention but giving that one special lady the attention she deserves. As I shared in an earlier chapter, trying to keep up and satisfy multiple women can be mentally exhausting.

Growing from a. Carless boy to a successful man meant that I chose my circle wisely. I don't entertain or hang out with just anyone.

My uncle Gerald's death was a huge eye opener when I was younger. You can't trust anyone, but instead trust your true feelings

Growing from a careless boy to a successful man meant that I stick to my word. If I say I'm going to do something, then that's exactly what I am going to do.

It's also an important trait I teach my daughters. Your word truly is your bond.

Growing from a careless boy to a successful man meant that I am okay with expressing myself and my feelings. Growing up, I had a hard time expressing myself and it was also taught that boys don't cry.

As I got older expressing myself was a very difficult thing to do. I learned this at my uncle's funeral.

Being able to express yourself as a man can resolve a lot of communication issues. By keeping things bottled and inside can be detrimental to yourself which is why it's important to vent and having the right people in your circle to keep you motivated.

As I look back over my entire life and the mistakes I've made, all that I can say is that God has truly blessed me because I'm still here. The future is bright and I look forward to continuing the journey of mentoring youth and becoming a law enforcement officer full time.

Writing my story was one thing. Sharing my story for the world to read was another thing. I took a risk by baring my soul on the pages of my first book but I did with one group in mind—young black youth.

Everyday I go to work in an environment with a group of teens that wants to be heard. I've mentored these boys over the years and while doing so it reminded how I was once them going down the wrong path by choice.

I wrote this book to share my journey with them and let them know they are not alone. I wanted to share a few gems I've learned over the years—I wanted to put them on game.

As a society, our young black men go through so much and sometimes it's hard to know if you are on the right path or not. I dedicated this book to all the youth I work with because I want them to know they are worth it and can be successful.

Just because you see images of black men getting killed all the time doesn't mean that has to be your future. I want my youth to know their future matters.

So what's next for me? I'm still pursuing a career in law enforcement and will move to the west coast to pursue it further.

Alongside continuing to pursue my career in law enforcement, I am still being the best father I can be two my beautiful daughters.

My father is still a high presence in my life and I listen to him much more now than I did when I was younger. Both of my parents have pursued a higher education and continuing to show what black love and excellence looks like.

My parents have been married more than twenty years and they both are a true inspiration of what love and marriage looks like. One day I hope to have what they have. Because of the relationship I witnessed between my parents, I now know what to look for in a woman.

My family inspired me to write this book. My life experiences have taught me so much and if I can help it, I want another young man to avoid the pitfalls I fell into.

My mentees also inspired me to write this book and for them and the bond we share, I am forever grateful.

In the meantime, I am more focused on my daughters, my

career and continuing to mentor my youth. I am proud of these boys and the future is bright for them.

Not only is the future bright for them, but it's bright for me as well and all I can do is go up from here.

With God on my side, all things are possible and for that, I'll forever be grateful for the change of going from a careless boy to a successful man.